WHAT ABOUT US?

FAMILIUS

Praise for *What About Us?*

"Karen Kleiman's wisdom about not only taking care of the mother and her well-being, but also her partner and their whole system at large, helps us all stay connected to our partners and loved ones during a tumultuous, life-changing, and potentially relationship-taxing time. . . . God bless Karen for her support in helping us all integrate every relationship within our 'new normal' as parents. Her humor, experience, wisdom, and insight are like a port in the most heart-spinning of storms."

—ALANIS MORISSETTE

"Parents often experience tension in their relationships after baby, but often have limited time to read about, reflect, and work through challenges. What About Us? is the answer parents have been waiting for. Through powerful, relatable visuals and Karen Kleiman's decades of experience working with families, partners now have an opportunity to see they're not alone and have a roadmap to move forward together."

—STEPHANIE GREUNKE, MS, RD, CPT, PMH-C

FAMILIUS

Published by Familius LLC, www.familius.com
PO Box 1249 Reedley, Ca 93654.
www.familius.com

Familius books are available at special discounts for bulk purchases,
whether for sales promotions or for family or corporate use.
For more information, email orders@familius.com.

Library of Congress Control Number: 2021935535

Print ISBN 978-1-64170-571-4
Ebook ISBN 978-1-64170-619-3
KF 978-1-64170-591-2
FE 978-1-64170-605-6

Printed in China

Edited by Lacey Wulf and Peg Sandkam
Cover design by Carlos Guerrero and Mara Harris
Book design by Mara Harris

10 9 8 7 6 5 4 3 2 1

First Edition

WHAT ABOUT US?

A New Parents Guide

to safeguard your over-anxious,
over-extended,
sleep-deprived relationship

KAREN KLEIMAN, MSW

ILLUSTRATIONS BY MOLLY MCINTYRE

Contents

Introduction........1

Chapter 1: This Is Us?........7

* A Wonderful Mess
* The Hormone Part
* Diaper Is Too Tight
* It's Expensive!
* Help You What?
* Please Find Me

Chapter 2: Here's What I'm Thinking........21

* No Good Timing
* I'm Pregnant and Freaking Out
* Sorry for What I Said When I Was Feeling Crappy
* PANIC!
* We Can't Lose This Pregnancy
* If I Snuggle, You Want Sex

Chapter 3: I Need You to Know This Hurts........35

* Postpartum Jiggles
* Seriously Don't Touch Me
* Don't Ask
* What Happened to My Vagina?
* Six-Week All Clear
* Why Aren't You Attracted to Me?

Chapter 4: Are We In This Together?.......49

* You Don't Understand
* Did the Baby Sleep Through the Night Again?
* No Time

* Why Don't We Talk?
* Baby Loves You More
* This Cannot Be Okay

Chapter 5: What If This Happens to Us?........63

* We Can't Get Pregnant?!
* Unplanned Pregnancy
* Unbearable Sadness

* Loss Is Forever
* Impossibly Difficult Circumstances

Chapter 6: Finding Us........75

* Remember When We Had a Life?
* When Compromise Feels Like Losing
* Negotiation Is an Art Form

* When Did We Become Our Parents?!
* Please Don't Touch the Baby
* I Want a Baby, You Want a Vasectomy

Chapter 7: The Power of Our Relationship........89

* OMG Put Your Phone Down Please
* He Needs a Hat

* I Think She's Hungry
* Wake Up Please
* Take the Baby!

Chapter 8: Mom Struggles........101

* Just Feed the Baby
* The World Can Be a Scary Place
* Actually, I Really Do Take Care of Everything
* If You Only Knew What I Was Thinking: Scary Thoughts
* Either Way, I Feel Guilty
* I Cannot Live This Way

Chapter 9: Dad Struggles........115

* What Are We Gonna Do?
* I Can't Get Those Images Out of My Head
* Could You Stop Telling Me What to Do and How to Do It?
* Am I Just Like My Dad?
* I Have to Stay Strong for My Family
* Would My Kids Be Better Off without Me?

Chapter 10: This Is Us Now........129

* When Worry Resides
* Are We Okay?
* Cultivating Resilience
* Finding Humor
* Revisit Your Circle of Affection

Resources........141

References........149

To All New Parents

"What happened to us?" we hear couples express woefully in therapy. "We used to be so carefree, so fun, so in love. Now, all we do is bicker and snap at each other."

When couples first navigate intimacy in a committed relationship, they generate something called a *circle of affection* (Kleiman, 2014). Imagine a circle that encompasses the two partners and all their individualities, predilections, desires, passions, and values. It's a circle that envelops the two of you and everything you enjoy and hope for. It's just "you and me." This circle connects you to each other with the promise of shared dreams and the challenge of potential struggles. The circle of affection is what keeps you tuned into each other, creating a protective bubble—despite the pull from external life forces, such as work, financial stress, loss, other dysfunctional relationships, just to name a few. This is where it has always been "all about us."

Partners do their best to sustain this connection by paying attention to the relationship. By taking care of each other. By listening to what is not being said out loud. By considering the needs of your partner, which at times take priority. Research shows that when couples attend to the needs of their partners, both individuals report greater happiness and longer-term satisfaction, thus nurturing and maintaining the circle of affection.

When we add a baby to this picture, the external stressors impacting the circle of affection intensify. Couples are often surprised to discover they may not have the skills to respond adaptively. When we factor in variables such as sleep deprivation, hormonal changes, predispositions to depression and anxiety, and different personalities, it's no wonder each individual in a partnership feels overwhelmed and stretched beyond capacity. The tension that emerges in response to the unrelenting demands and stressors can be misinterpreted as a sign that something is either wrong with the relationship or that the baby is coming between them. While all emotions are heightened during this major life transition, anxiety especially runs rampant and, if left unchecked, can rapidly accelerate, leaving new parents feeling unsupported and downright miserable.

The addition of a baby is as disruptive as it is exhilarating. As couples are thrust into the demanding task of caring for a newborn, they find little or no time to attend to their relationship. Tedious tasks replace romantic gestures; chats about bodily functions are the new center of intimacy. Couples often find themselves lost in the busyness. The urgency of caring for an infant transcends anything and everything. Any reference to or silent wondering *What about us?* leads to the same answer: *We have to wait.* Consequently, the relationship is put on the back burner. *Wait until we get some sleep. Wait until I can hear myself think. Wait until I can take a shower without someone screaming my name. Wait, I can only do so much at one time. WAIT.* Withstanding the strain of 24/7 baby care, the relationship often takes a huge hit, no matter how loving, no matter how connected, no matter how well-intended. It makes sense that partners are preoccupied and can only focus on the adorable tumult inundating their senses. Nonetheless, amidst the excitement and the unpredictable stressors, one or both of the partners can suddenly feel overwhelmed and utterly alone.

Research has taught us that this primary relationship must be attended to, especially during times of high stress. It has been shown that a whopping 67 percent of new parents experience conflict, disappointment, and hurt feelings after having a baby (Gottman, 2008). When comparing couples with and without children, research shows the rate of decline in relationship satisfaction is nearly twice the rate for couples who have children than for childless couples (Doss et al., 2009). Moreover, a poor marital relationship is the most consistent psychosocial predictor of postpartum depression (Beck, 2001). Support from a partner can actually protect against depression in both mothers and fathers. Even without the presence of a clinical depression or anxiety disorder, both men and women are vulnerable to substantial anxiety, which can interfere with the best-laid plans.

Our vision for *What About Us?* is to teach you how to adapt to this unprecedented stress by providing skills aimed at reinforcing your circle of affection and helping you tap into your strengths as a couple. Consistent with our first book, *Good Moms Have Scary Thoughts*, each page will have a comic depicting a common stressor, followed by text, which will describe and validate the issue the couple is confronting, along with a journal doodle offering specific skill-building exercises. This book provides evidenced-based solutions to areas of vulnerability or conflict that can arise during the perinatal period (i.e., pregnancy and postpartum) and support for stress that is hard to put into words. We are hopeful that this resource will help you take care of your relationship while you are so busy taking care of everything else.

#speakthesecret

Chapter 1

....

This Is Us?

A Wonderful Mess

Having a baby is hard on a relationship. It seems that no matter how much they prepare, couples are often stunned by the absolute chaos that quickly descends upon them. While it's hard to prepare for sleeplessness and ear-piercing cries, couples that anticipate some degree of turmoil seem to cope better, with less bitterness and greater satisfaction, than those who feel blindsided. Alongside the excitement, constant worries and bickering will test your relationship like never before. Lack of sleep and short tempers can lead to snapping, blaming, and all kinds of resentments. Still, relationships can endure high levels of stress when they are fortified by mutual support and attention. Understanding and talking about the fact that this life transition will substantially impact your relationship are the first steps toward protecting it.

4 Keys to keep your partnership Steady

Lean into the relationship

Lean away from the chaos

Stay connected

pay attention to the needs of your partner

The Hormone Part

The first few days and weeks home with a new baby can be exhilarating, exhausting, and besieged by unknowns. We know that changes in mood can be linked to specific hormonal shifts in women, such as drops in estrogen and progesterone levels, which can lead to a roller coaster of emotions. While hormonal changes in male partners have been less studied, research shows that higher testosterone levels might protect against paternal depression, though it may increase relationship distress and dissatisfaction. Whether it is hormonal or situational, both partners can initially feel on the verge of crying or lashing out. This is a good time to remind yourself that, whether or not this is your first child, you are both adjusting and you are both on the same team.

Sometimes, the best you can do is let your partner know that their feelings are okay. Remember that being kind to each other, especially when it feels hard to do so, is more important than you might realize.

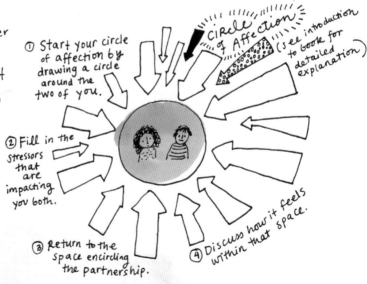

① Start your circle of affection by drawing a circle around the two of you.

Circle of Affection (see introduction to book for detailed explanation)

② Fill in the stressors that are impacting you both.

③ Return to the space encircling the partnership.

④ Discuss how it feels within that space.

Diaper Is Too Tight

It's hard to relinquish the primary caregiving role. Moms often feel that their maternal instincts take precedence when it comes to meeting the needs of a new baby. But there's a lot to do, and sharing the responsibilities is crucial. While there are obvious tasks that scream for attention, the majority of what needs attention is invisible—the emotional load, the ever-evolving division of labor, overall well-being of the family, the management and coordination of all of these aspects, and the foresight to anticipate what needs to be done before it needs to be done. Sometimes, it is tempting for one partner to take the lead in overseeing the execution of these tasks. However, it's important for both partners to stay involved and recognize that they each own what needs to be done. Shared ownership requires letting go of the expectation that a task will be done your way. Trust that your partner will take care of things, even if their way is not the same as yours. Remember that partners need to spend time alone with the baby, without criticism, judgment, or scrutiny. When you feel the urge to offer your advice, take a deep breath and walk away. Believe in your partner's ability to learn through their own efforts.

TRY This: If there is a childcare task that needs attention, talk about the specifics.

Let's talk about _____.
I would feel better if you _____ instead of _____.
That's because when you _____, sometimes it makes me _____.
Does this work for you?
Is there something I'm doing that you would like me to do differently?

Let's talk about _____.
I would feel better if you _____ instead of _____.
That's because when you _____, sometimes it makes me _____.
Does this work for you?
Is there something I'm doing that you would like me to do differently?

It's Expensive!

The financial weight of raising a baby is real, and costs add up quickly. This can create immeasurable stress for the couple, even before the baby comes. One of you might stay home with the baby, or you may choose another arrangement that alters your income, and this can add tension to your relationship and to your finances. The high price tag of parenthood forces families to pay close attention to the tension between work and family life choices with the goal of finding a balance that feels right for everyone. Often, partners disagree on what is an appropriate amount of money to spend on items for the baby, especially when considering that babies only truly need a few things to keep them safe and healthy.

Talk with your partner about which items matter to you and why spending more on certain things is important. Then, work together to find alternate ways to secure items that you need, or want, for your baby.

☐ Determine your baby budget.

☐ Make separate lists for one-time expenses (ex: giving birth), gear expenses (ex: car seats), & routine expenses (ex: diapers).

☐ Prioritize your spending together— sometimes spending is emotional; share emotional reasons for valuing one item highly.

☐ Find ways to share baby items. Social media has tons of ways to find other parents eager to share their baby's gently used items for low or zero cost!

16

Help You What?

When couples are overwhelmed, emotions run wild and communication can break down. Each of you can quickly feel dismissed and misunderstood, disappointed that the other does not just know what is needed. Consequently, you may want to wait-and-see if your partner will figure out what you need and actually help. But this approach can leave you feeling abandoned and alone. One tactic, which might sound counterintuitive at first, to help your partner meet your needs is for *you to give first*. When you start by acknowledging the emotional state of your partner, you actually help them help *you*, by nudging them closer to you. This way, they feel more understood and are less likely to criticize or retreat. Also, when you ask for help from your partner, be specific and identify any obstacles that may get in the way.

First state something that will feel supportive to your partner, then ask for what you need.

- I know you are tired, **BUT** do you mind helping me with _____.

- **AFTER** you take a few minutes to decompress, can you please _____.

- **THANK YOU** for everything you're doing, can you **please** help with one more thing?

Please Find Me

Sometimes the combination of unprecedented anxiety, responsibility of a newborn, and overwhelming expectations leads to a disruption of everything you love about your relationship. As you both are thrust into the demands of caring for a newborn, you find limited time to attend to your relationship. Menial tasks replace romantic gestures and discussions about bodily functions are commonplace. The urgency of caring for an infant transcends anything and everything. Often, the relationship gets put on the back burner. This primary relationship, your partnership, and the connection that drives it must be attended to, especially during times of high stress. As tempting as it may be to set it aside while you scramble to take care of everything else, holding your relationship in the forefront will make everything else feel more doable. So a good place to start is to muster your energy and have a heart-to-heart about what you need from each other.

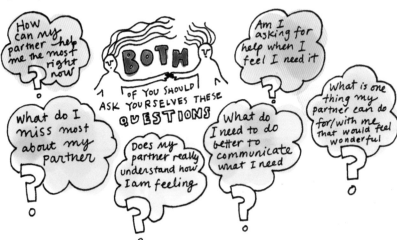

BOTH OF YOU SHOULD ASK YOURSELVES THESE QUESTIONS

How can my partner help me the most right now

Am I asking for help when I feel I need it

What is one thing my partner can do for/with me that would feel wonderful

What do I miss most about my partner

Does my partner really understand how I am feeling

What do I need to do better to communicate what I need

Chapter 2

Here's What I'm Thinking

Yikes. A baby. We can hardly do US! Am I mature enough? Am I old enough? Do I feel pressured to do this? How do I know if it's really what I want or what I THINK I should want?
Do you think it's time we talk about having a baby? We said we would start when we got married.
Really?
Gah. Now? Us? Parents? Really? Are we ready? Can we afford it? I don't think we have enough money.... A baby. Me, a dad. Wow. What? I dunno. What do we have to give up? Sleep? going out? Fun? Argh.

No Good Timing

When considering having a baby, conversations and practical decisions need to take place about important issues—religion, finances, strength of the relationship, parental leave policies, to name a few. At the earliest stages, what's most important is for you to sit down as a couple, with few distractions, and begin to explore your feelings about having a baby. These discussions should focus on your expectations, your fears and worries, and what excites you. While your "plans" may be sidelined by life events and unforeseen interferences, you will feel more in control if you come up with a general timeline that feels right to both of you. It is normal to be nervous or confused about this life-altering decision. The best approach when tackling difficult conversations is to be open and straightforward about your positive and negative thoughts and emotions.

I'm Pregnant and Freaking Out

So many rules. So many opinions about what to do and what not to do. So much pressure to do it the "right" way. Input from healthcare providers can contradict what family and friends say, not to mention what drops on social media. The anxiety can mislead you into thinking you are not cut out for having a baby. You need to protect yourself from too many unsolicited viewpoints. First, find a safe person, someone you trust to understand how you feel and give honest feedback based on your best interests. Try to stick with decisions and practices that align with your worries, fears, and hopes, and those of your partner, healthcare provider, and designated safe person. Second, set boundaries with friends and family members; this will reduce the anxiety of too much conflicting information being thrust upon you. Third, limit your time on social media, as tempted as you may be for the support and guidance. Excessive scrolling is not good for anxiety, and it is not good for your relationship.

In addition to my partner, my safe person is: ____

One good way for me to set a boundary right now is: ____

The web-based resources I will focus on reading are: ____

If I need help identifying my safe person, a boundary, or a reliable resource, I can ask ____ to help me with this.

Sorry for What I Said
When I Was Feeling Crappy

Moodiness, nausea, overstimulation, and sleep deprivation are part of pregnancy and parenthood. Sometimes, it's hard to be kind when you are not feeling like your best and healthiest self. Your biggest enemy right now is the lack of filter that comes with feeling depleted. If you inadvertently say something hurtful to your partner, the first step toward repair is to acknowledge your behavior. Then put down all devices. Good communication requires attention, eye contact, and intentional listening skills. While it may feel difficult, it is important that you focus on each other with as much patience and presence as you can round up. Even though the baby feels like your only priority, neglecting your relationship will leave you feeling weary, less supported, and less capable as you face the challenges ahead.

12 tips for good communication

DO

- Find the right time & place for talking.
- Use "I" statements rather than "you."
- Listen well.
- Maintain eye contact.
- Be honest & direct.
- Express yourself with clarity & support.
- Focus on the present issue.
- Check your tone & the words you use.
- Begin with a statement of good will.
- Acknowledge how your partner might be feeling.
- Give your partner the benefit of the doubt.
- Take a time-out if needed.

DON'T

- Assume
- Blame
- Judge
- Use words like "always" & "never."
- Do all the talking.
- Insist on having the last word.
- Interrupt.
- Jump to conclusions
- Be sarcastic
- Walk away
- Roll your eyes
- Play the martyr

28

PANIC!

Health anxiety is very common during the perinatal period. Sometimes anxiety can get so high that thoughts about your own well-being overshadow everything else. You might obsess about your heart rate or other bodily symptoms like a spot, mark, lump, or feeling that you swear wasn't there yesterday, convincing yourself that you have a serious medical condition. Grounding exercises and mindful breathing can help you refocus attention to the here and now and activate the parasympathetic, or calming part, of the nervous system. To ground yourself, concentrate on something around you—sights, sounds, smells—in your immediate environment. Then breathe in for four counts, hold for four counts, and breathe out for five counts. Mindful breathing has been shown to increase oxygen flow to the brain and signal the nervous system to relax, even when you don't do anything else! Find an app (see page 147) that can help regulate your breathing. With regular practice of grounding and mindful breathing, your anxiety is likely to subside.

What area of concern can you try to manage on your own with self-care? _____

What area of concern do you think you need to discuss with your doctor?

_____

We Can't Lose This Pregnancy

Any previous loss through miscarriage, ectopic pregnancy, stillbirth, or infant death can present an unimaginable life crisis for couples. Even close friends and family cannot fully grasp the emotional toll experienced by this devastation, and they may unintentionally express sentiments that are unhelpful, such as presuming this pregnancy will magically heal the pain. Planning or experiencing another pregnancy can conjure mixed feelings such as guilt and joy. While getting pregnant after a loss is a cherished relief, many women say that the anxiety of another loss makes it hard to connect to this new pregnancy. Try to prepare yourself by expecting these complicated and conflicting emotions. It is normal to feel both cautiously optimistic and restrained. Be gentle with yourself.

Sit with your partner & list positive & negative emotions about this current pregnancy. Read them aloud to each other. Then tell your partner one thing they can do to help you with each negative emotion.

EX: Anxiety ➡ REMIND ME THAT EVERYTHING IS GOING TO BE OKAY.

If I Snuggle, You Want Sex

Relationships thrive when intimacy is strong. When sexual intimacy is compromised or postponed, it becomes even more important to nurture other means of maintaining closeness. Finding ways to connect physically and emotionally can feel rewarding and satisfying for couples who are overloaded and exhausted. However, loving gestures can be misconstrued. Partners might worry about the (intentional or unintentional) initiation of sex and, therefore, retreat. These worries should be clearly communicated to reduce the likelihood of misinterpretation or hurt feelings. When possible, take steps to remain physically close by sitting together, snuggling, hugging, kissing, laughing, and touching, so long as both of you remain clear about the intentions and expectations involved. Spend time alone without your baby, if possible, even if you can only grab a moment here and there. Heartfelt compliments to your partner can remind you of the foundation of your initial attraction. Remember who you both are and who you were before the baby.

Chapter 3

I Need You to Know This Hurts

36

Postpartum Jiggles

Even when a partner perceives a postpartum body or parent-bod as attractive, these changes in physique may be experienced as shameful. Of course, partners think they are helping by flattering and expressing feelings of attraction or desire. While some new mothers do embrace the changes brought on by this magnificent achievement of childbirth and view these physical changes as a badge of honor, it is normal to need time to adjust to feeling at home in her new body. Talking about this can be comforting for some and triggering for others. This hard conversation is better off led by the partner experiencing this discomfort. As the partner offering support, remember to do so by listening with a tender and open heart.

1. I made a baby!

2. I so rock!

3. I will focus on my strengths

4. I appreciate & respect what my body has been through

5. I will try to stay out of my head

PLEDGE TO MY POSTPARTUM BODY

6. I understand that I am probably expecting too much from myself right now

7. I trust the process & will give myself time

8. Welcome to the new sexy!

9. _____

10. _____

38

Seriously Don't Touch Me

There are many reasons why a postpartum woman might shrink away from touch. Some refer to this as feeling "touched out." It isn't only about physical touch. It can also be code for feeling weary from what is perceived as a steady stream of neediness, dependence, or total reliance on her for nurturance and attention. Or it could simply be a reflexive response. Perhaps she has a looming fear of getting pregnant again, which may unintentionally create a desire for even more physical distance. It can be a reminder that she is still recovering and adjusting to the changes in her heart, her mind, and her body. It may represent a longing for her pre-pregnant state or an eagerness to establish a positive relationship with her body. The point is she needs a break. Pushing through this reaction without asking or listening to what she needs can set everyone up for disappointment. Physical and emotional accommodations during the postpartum period take time, love, and kindness from both of you.

39

Don't Ask

As many as one-third of women who give birth, vaginally or by Caesarian (C-) section, experience some degree of pelvic floor dysfunction or organ prolapse, which can create significant discomfort, urinary and bowel problems, and painful sex. Sometimes, when the pelvic floor muscles are weakened from pregnancy or delivery, the uterus can begin to slide down into the vagina. Be sure to contact your healthcare provider if you have uncomfortable physical symptoms that disrupt your normal activities. Strengthening of the pelvic floor muscles (e.g., via Kegel exercises) is important for all postpartum women, even those without prolapse. Oftentimes, physical therapy can help. In the meantime, try to keep the dialogue open between you and your partner.

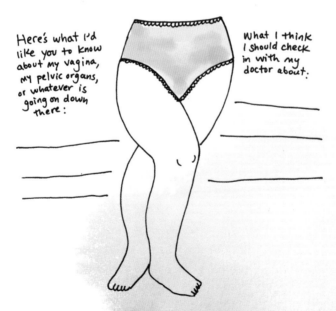

Here's what I'd like you to know about my vagina, my pelvic organs, or whatever is going on down there:

What I think I should check in with my doctor about:

What Happened to My Vagina?

If you've had a vaginal birth, let's face it, your vagina will be sore. And possibly, the perineum (the area between your vagina and anus) as well. Tears or lacerations may or may not require stitches, usually healing within a few weeks. Fourth-degree tears, which affect the perineal muscles and rectal tissue, are the most serious and often need to be surgically repaired. Women who deliver by C-section may have incision and pelvic pain and can even experience vaginal pain. All of these factors (and more!) will contribute to Mom not being in the mood, emotionally or physically, for sexual activity to resume until she feels better. While this waiting period may feel prolonged or disappointing to one or both of you, keep in mind that this is not just about physical pain. This is a time when both of you are adapting to considerable life changes and learning to trust each other and the process of recovery. Take it slow. Discomfort should ease as healing continues. Talk about it. Remember, your medical providers are there to offer guidance even after your postpartum follow-up appointment.

Do not let feelings of shame or embarrasment stop you from saying what you need to your partner & to your healthcare provider.

the Antidote to shame is self-compassion (you) & empathy (partner)

Six-Week All Clear

Not feeling ready for sex? Too sore? Too dry? Not in the mood? Rocking, feeding, holding all day? Needing some space? Getting the medical green light doesn't always translate into individual readiness. Sometimes, for women who are eager to resume "normal activities," it does. But for a majority of women, recovery and desire are slower to return. Everyone is different. Cultural, social, and personal expectations can add pressure to have sex after childbirth, which can lead to discontentment on both sides. As the sexual relationship adapts to the new baby environment, both partners need to be truthful and open about their fears and desires to avoid upsetting each other. When you are both ready (or before you are both ready), have the conversation. Remember, it might help to have a professional normalize this experience. You can say, "My midwife (doula, doctor, therapist, nurse, etc.) said it is super common for postpartum women to not be interested in sex." Set your own timeline. Together.

1. Let's sit down & talk about my appointment today.

2. Everything is good. I know you are hoping that means we have been cleared to have sex. I'm getting there.

3. I think I would feel better if I could tell you some of the things I'm afraid of.

4. Do you think we could discuss ways to be intimate without intercourse for now?

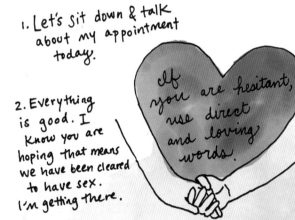

If you are hesitant, use direct and loving words.

Why Aren't You Attracted to Me?

Some partners find the blooming belly to be exciting and sexually arousing. Others express a more tentative response and may be afraid for the baby's safety during intimacy or intercourse. Still others find the pregnancy body to be a total turn-off. Research indicates that some men have a drop in testosterone levels after the birth of a baby, perhaps to prepare them for childcare responsibilities and also dial down their desire for sex. These factors may collide or align with Mom's own efforts to come to terms with her changing shape and body image. As always, talking about these issues makes dealing with them more productive. The benefit of a supportive partner is indisputable and highly predictive of more satisfying relationships.

Intimacy means different things to everyone and involves the way two partners stay close and connected, even if it's not through sex. It is not just a question of *being* supportive. Both partners need to *perceive* the relationship as supportive. Without this, they are at an increased risk for depression and anxiety during pregnancy and after the baby arrives.

...support can be practical (making dinner) and it can be emotional (I am here for you)

Emotional SUPPORT tips

1) Non-verbal contact
2) Loving body language
3) Must be unconditional
4) Use touch
5) Provide words of reassurance
6) Follow up if you say you will do something
7) Take a pregnancy/postpartum class together
8) Check in — then check in again later

Chapter 4

Are We
In This
Together?

You Don't Understand

Some new parents say they don't even know how to talk to each other anymore. One woman described it like this: "It feels like he misunderstands everything I say. He gets mad when I tell him how to do something. Then he gets mad if I let him do it by himself. Either way, we fight about it." Misunderstandings can be the simple result of exhaustion or be more complicated. While a new baby certainly brings major stress, in some relationships this stress can evolve in an adaptive manner without disrupting the core relationship. In others, high levels of stress can be associated with greater unhappiness or impaired functioning within the partnership. In fact, John Gottman reveals that 67 percent of couples report marital dissatisfaction during the first three years after having a baby! Fighting in a relationship isn't a problem, but how you fight can be. As satisfaction declines, hostility, resentment, and feelings of isolation can creep in. The two of you should focus on ways to manage the inescapable stress, while protecting your relationship from negativity. Learning how to express yourself in ways that will not hurt your partner or attack their character will help you problem solve more successfully.

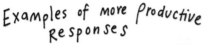

Examples of more Productive Responses

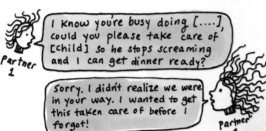

Partner 1: I know you're busy doing [....], could you please take care of [child] so he stops screaming and I can get dinner ready?

Partner 2: Sorry, I didn't realize we were in your way. I wanted to get this taken care of before I forgot!

Ask Yourself:

- Am I really listening?
- Do I try to understand what my partner is saying/asking?
- Do I express myself with clarity?
- Do my emotions get in the way of my speaking clearly?
- Am I provocative when I talk?
- Am I thinking about how my partner feels?

51

Did the Baby Sleep Through the Night Again?

While new babies often sleep a lot, they also wake up a lot, leaving both parents exhausted. If one parent is breastfeeding, it may seem obvious that she is the one who needs to get up multiple times throughout the night. But this can be maddening for the partner who is awake and alone night after night. One way to curtail resentment is to share the post-feeding tasks (e.g., burping, changing diapers or clothes). Any kind of help in the middle of the night can feel extremely supportive. Some couples decide to alternate nights or split each night. If one of you works outside the home, you might want to split the nighttime duties into weekdays and weekends, especially if the baby starts taking a bottle. Remember that no matter what seems to work best for you, even meticulous plans turn upside down, which allows frustrations to surge. If something isn't working and sleep deprivation is winning, ask for help. Everything feels and is easier when you get sleep. During the postpartum period, adequate sleep is essential, so make sure to reconfigure the landscape if your precious baby is creating consecutive sleepless nights.

Let's discuss our night time routine

IS IT WORKING THE WAY IT IS ???

DOES IT FEEL FAIR TO BOTH OF US ??

IF NOT, HOW SHOULD WE MODIFY IT? WHY?

Let's agree to try this too:

1) _____ 2) _____ 3) _____

No Time

Happier relationships are more forgiving and tolerant of both partners' mistakes, faults, and vulnerabilities. Partners view the problem as situational (e.g., he's in such a bad mood), rather than personality flaws or characteristics (e.g., he's so lazy). When two individuals come together with two sets of expectations and priorities, having a baby can accentuate their differences. As these differences settle in, couples might find they are defaulting to roles and responsibilities that don't always feel fair. Open communication with a mutual problem-solving goal is necessary. Your partner might not always place the same importance on a particular task that you do. Remember, you are learning how to accept the presence of some very strong emotions. You can increase tolerance by clarifying your position, balancing gender norms and expectations, and listening carefully to your partner's concerns.

PAUSE before you REACT. Breathe. Wait. Say what you need to say with kindness.

Why Don't We Talk?

Experts have both confirmed and disproven long-held gender stereotypes about how men and women communicate (e.g., women talk more than men, women use language to connect, men use language to inform or accomplish something). None of these stereotypes, however, are relevant when it comes to real people and the serious need for clear and supportive communication. What does seem to hold true is that, if one partner is with the baby all day and the other partner works outside the home, there can be a mismatch of colliding expectations and decompression styles. In the first moment of quiet amid conflict, some partners go silent or "shut down." Others seek emotional connection through voicing feelings. When partners with differing styles of communication are overwhelmed, these differences can create an impasse, which needs attending so that individual coping responses are not misinterpreted as anger or disconnect. If a fight ensues and turns unproductive or spiteful, then take a break and resume the discussion once emotions are less volatile.

What I tend to do when I get overwhelmed: _____

How you respond: _____
How I'd like you to respond: _____

What You tend to do when you get overwhelmed: _____

How I respond: _____
How you'd like me to respond: _____

The two of them are so in love, it's like I'm not even here. They don't need me. I know that's not true, but that's how it feels. I'm like a third wheel.

Baby Loves You More

From time to time, amid the all-consuming, real-life tumult, one (or both) of you might be surprised to find yourself jealous of the baby or of your partner. You might envy the baby for taking up so much of your partner's time and energy or believe the baby loves your partner more than you. While these feelings are totally understandable in light of the abrupt shift in doting attention, it may help to hear that they are growing pains, of sorts. As parental roles evolve to be more balanced, primary caregiving may temporarily reside with one partner at a time (e.g., the one feeding or staying at home), leaving the other feeling marginalized. While feelings of jealousy are common, if left unchecked, ongoing pangs can lead to feelings of resentment, mistrust, sadness, or abandonment. In some cases, extreme jealousy may be the expression of insecure and possessive personality traits. Any area of instability in your relationship that predated the baby's arrival can negatively impact your new family dynamics, so pay attention to hot spots in the partnership.

Create your sanctuary

where? _____
when? _____
why? _____
Rules? _____
Name? _____

60

This Cannot Be Okay

Disagreements, arguments, disappointments, and hurt feelings are inevitable as the two of you traverse this territory. As tempting as it might be, it is rarely a good idea to avoid addressing big emotions that are getting in the way. Solid relationships can sustain high levels of distress. The key strategy is to identify the potential standstill, share perspectives, and problem solve along the way. When strong feelings of disconnect emerge, the partner who is most concerned, most affected, or most motivated to repair the injury may raise the issue—a call to attention for both partners. When feelings of hurt or detachment are ignored, longer-term disregard for each other can embed itself within your relationship. If progress in resolving an issue feels blocked, take a break and revisit it later with a clear head.

CONVERSATION STARTERS

are we okay?

this doesn't feel good to me. Let's find a time to talk.

You seem upset. I'm upset. Let's make time to address what's going on.

I feel like we are going through the motions. Want to talk about this?

I know this is hard. I think it's important we talk about what's going on.

Chapter 5

What If This Happens to Us?

We Can't Get Pregnant?!

There are so many stressors related to infertility—financial worries, side effects from medications and interventions, the agony of treatment failures, ongoing psychological grief and distress, and misguided opinions from loved ones with good intentions, to name a few. When a friend wants to celebrate her own good fortune, you may notice your emotions range from wanting to share in her joy and wanting to shrink away and vanish. The complex emotions can leave a couple with feelings of envy, shame, and bitterness and feeling isolated by their vulnerable state. It can even create self-interested and scary thoughts that are hard to admit out loud, which can be excruciatingly painful. Hopefully, friends will understand this is a delicate situation and will give you the space, grace, and understanding you need and deserve. Your partner may or may not align with your thinking. As always, approach each other with care and respect. Empathy is key to finding relief from the suffering.

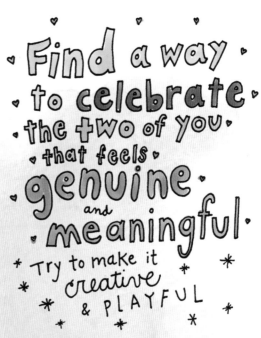

Find a way to celebrate the two of you that feels genuine and meaningful. Try to make it creative & PLAYFUL

Unplanned Pregnancy

Surprises happen. They can happen to people who are very cautious and conscientious, including parents who use contraceptives responsibly. When unplanned pregnancy happens, it is normal to experience a wide range of intense emotions, including some negative or uncomfortable. Acknowledge any feelings of joy or excitement you might have as well as feelings of shock, fear, or panic that you might also experience. Take care of yourself and your partner* emotionally and, when the most intense emotions subside a bit, begin to think rationally. Who can be part of your decision-making team? Should you contact a healthcare provider? Explore the pros and cons of expanding your family. Ask your partner how you can support them, and share your top positive and negative emotions, top priority, and fears about the pregnancy.

*If you do not have a partner, an unintended pregnancy can be particularly challenging. Make sure you are informed and seek out support from safe and non-judgmental sources.

Your top
Negative Emotions
1. _____
2. _____
3. _____

Partner's top
Negative Emotions (ask!)
1. _____
2. _____
3. _____

_____
what do we need to
figure out first?

Unbearable Sadness

Although one in four people experience miscarriage, as a culture we tend not to share these experiences with each other. Slowly, this is evolving in the right direction. Understanding miscarriage—what it is, what it feels like, how we know it has happened, what causes it, what actually happens during a miscarriage, and what it means for future fertility and pregnancies—is a part of having a baby that most couples don't know a lot about unless it happens to them. Ask questions of each other, ask questions of your medical care providers, and seek support from a counselor or friend whom you trust. Make room for grief. Everyone processes this loss differently. You may be surprised by how unaffected or non-reactive you feel, or you may find yourself completely overcome by strong emotions. You have lost a loved one. Any emotion you each experience is normal and valid. Recognize that now, more than ever, you need to listen with compassion and express your needs honestly to care for yourself and each other.

Here's how you will know if I am sad & here's something you can do to help when I am sad:

_____

_____

Here's how I will know if you are sad & here's something I can do to help when you are sad:

_____

_____

Loss is Forever

Nothing you did made this happen. Nothing you thought or said made this happen. No amount of answers will make this okay. You will not be okay for a while. It is important to know that, although the memory of your baby and the grief you are experiencing will stay with you, your sadness will not always feel so heavy and burdensome to carry. Also, keep in mind that each individual experiences grief differently and will show grief in different ways. If you are unsure about how your partner is feeling, ask. It is also important for you to share your own feelings with your partner and other people you trust.

Impossibly Difficult Circumstances

Most couples hope for the best, despite the outrageous amount of anxiety they feel individually. Any deviation from a healthy pregnancy or birth from what you expected and hoped for—regarding your birth plan, your pregnancy, your delivery, and your baby's well-being—is what we call an unexpected outcome. Discovering that your baby may have complications, an illness, or diagnosis is terrifying beyond description. No one can prepare for this, and people often find themselves imagining the worst possible scenario. The unknown is often the most difficult to deal with, so do your best to get accurate information. You have a right to expect clear communication from your provider, as well as compassion and guidance throughout this process. If possible, both of you should attend doctor visits together to make sure you are both informed and in agreement. Be sure to make the time to privately discuss your fears, your expectations, and your capacity to get through any challenge so long as you are strong together. Expand your village and seek support from extended family when feasible.

When life challenges us, we will be okay, because you are really good at

_____

I am really good at _____

When life is hard
I need you to _____
I can help you best by _____

Chapter 6

Finding Us

Remember When We Had a Life?

Parents often express guilt over missing the parts of their lives that have disappeared since having children. While deep in the new-baby trenches, you might be surprised to find an ache in your heart for your partner, even though they are right there with you. While your alone time as a couple feels out of reach, mundane obligations can take the place of romantic date nights. The loss of the private, personal connection between the two of you can make you feel unexpectedly sad. Or you might long for your before-baby experiences, such as impulsive outings, dinner for two, or cuddling on the couch in front of the TV. Indeed, it is incredibly hard to give proper attention to a relationship when there is a new baby in the picture. Nevertheless, when the desire to attend to the partnership gains traction, the relationship is fortified. Research literature is very clear that couples who take care of their relationship by taking care of each other will experience more joy and less conflict for a longer period of time.

Your Relationship will *thrive* in direct proportion to the amount of attention You give it

When Compromise Feels Like Losing

Any time there is a change to a family system, it can be challenging for everyone to understand their role in this new system. Part of that adjustment involves the establishment of boundaries in order to sustain healthy relationships. This goes for your partnership and your extended families. Sometimes, that transition goes fairly smoothly; sometimes, it does not. What's most important here is that the two of you work hard to remain in agreement for the most part. As a couple, unify your expectations and establish your narrative from the outset. If the two of you accept the boundaries that need to be established and maintained, then compromise can follow. If you find yourself blaming, keeping score, wanting credit, or taking the other for granted, you offset the equilibrium and appear as if you do not believe in your partnership, even if you do.

What is one thing you might do differently, in order to protect your relationship & establish a better boundary when it comes to others (in-laws? friends?)

_____

Negotiation is an Artform

With so many changes, compromises, and concessions, interactions can begin to feel like you are bartering for what you want and need. And to some extent, you are. After all, isn't that what healthy negotiation is all about? I give something to you, you give something to me. Conflict in a relationship is unavoidable. It is helpful to approach disagreements as normal events without a winner or a loser. Always talk it out. Make your position clear without yelling or screaming. Watch your language and your tone. Remember you are both winners if you navigate this well. Good, productive negotiating creates the opportunity for you to act as a team while allowing each of you to state your case, with clarity and consideration for the other.

Do you remember a time when you both felt overwhelmed, tense & stressed, & can recall it as a good example of when you both leaned in toward each other for support?

What did you need & appreciate the most?

When Did We Become Our Parents?!

Are we setting ourselves up for failure? It has been shown that babies tend to develop on track, regardless of what decisions, traditions, value system, or cultural influences inform parental interactions. Families of origin can have huge influences on your parenting choices. Patterns do trickle down from our parents, and you might find yourselves leaning towards some of your own parents' styles because this is what is familiar to you. Remember there is never one right way. In most instances, you might both be a little bit right, and it probably doesn't matter in the long run as much as you may think. If you see something played out by your partner that reminds you of their parent, it might incite a negative reaction. Adding fuel to the fire by bringing up issues or attitudes about, or over-identification with, in-laws will unequivocally not help. Harmony is best achieved by understanding the advantages of both of your parenting choices and inclinations. It's okay to agree to disagree, especially if you continue to support each other's position. Depending on the situation, most differences in responses will eventually lead to a new style that combines both of your preferences. In all cases, compromise involves seeking balance despite divergent views and adapting your values to the needs of your child.

Please Don't Touch the Baby

Sometimes it can be hard to distinguish between a common worry that causes reasonable boundaries from those that result from excessive anxiety, which can take on an obsessive quality and lead to controlling and perfectionistic behaviors. When the health or safety of the baby is concerned, it can be especially hard to distinguish anxious thoughts from rational fears. This is when it becomes important to assess whether you are able to push through the anxiety and "let go" or if you need to pay attention and stick with your gut instinct. When this is hard to untangle, your partner's objectivity might help you determine whether a particular limit you set is a result of your distress, which requires information or reassurance, or whether it is a realistic boundary that should be respected.

Write an example of what you perceive as a legitimate boundary but your partner perceives it as anxiety-driven or excessive.

When it comes to decisions about the baby, sometimes I prefer that we _____
And you think I'm being too _____
But I think you're being too _____
Maybe we can compromise by _____

I Want a Baby, You Want a Vasectomy

It can feel as though compromise is not possible when one of you feels that your family is complete and the other desires another baby. There is no right or wrong here. There is your viewpoint, my viewpoint, and our viewpoint. First, know you both can move forward together, strong emotions and all; you will be more effective if you make your points without the passionate undertones. Second, talk it out, listen hard, and take a break if necessary. Then, talk it out some more. Third, be respectful of all options and pay close attention to why your partner opposes your position. Clear decision making in the midst of gridlock is central to a healthy relationship. Feeling valued and heard is paramount. When you both can operate as if your partner's decision is as important as your own, you are building trust and enhancing your connection.

Solving the problem is not the ultimate objective. Having this open, supportive dialogue, and understanding your differences with compassion and gratitude, is the first step toward the solution.

Is there anything about your position of this dialogue that you feel is not being sufficiently heard? _____

What is your main priority that you want to get across? _____

Chapter 7

The Power of Our Relationship

OMG Put Your Phone Down Please

Sometimes both partners can get caught up in the constant stimulation and competing demands for attention. Everyone needs something now! Add a baby or toddler to the mix and everything seems to get louder, busier, and harder. The best response to this sensory overload is to shut it down by trying hard not to react or initiate a new request in the moment because it will likely fall upon deaf ears. Instead, disengage. Get out of there. State a neutral comment to excuse yourself (e.g., I'll be back in a few minutes); then, leave the room. Temporarily disengaging is important if you consider yourself to be highly sensitive and are unsettled by too much sensory input. No good can come from trying to out-talk each other. You both will likely overreact and misread what is needed. Separating yourself from the tense moment can help you recharge and gather your thoughts, which is hard to do in the midst of family commotion. Take a break and reunite after some deep breaths.

Safe Exit Agreement

It is okay to remove ourselves if things feel like too much.
We are not abandoning each other. We are taking care of ourselves & we will agree to return as soon as we refresh so we can resolve the issue at hand.

Here is what I'm going to say to remove myself from the discussion temporarily:

Here is what you're going to say if you need to remove yourself from the discussion temporarily:

He Needs a Hat

A truly supportive partnership can strengthen or break the backbone of this vulnerable period in the life of a relationship. Supporting each other doesn't mean you both agree. It means that the integrity of your relationship transcends the details of who is right or who needs to yield at any particular time. It means creating and sustaining clear boundaries, especially when a third party like an in-law is involved. As a parent, you are already bombarded with misgivings, hesitation, and lack of a direction, and the situation will not improve with someone you perceive as meddling or overly opinionated, however well-intentioned they may be. Loyalty to the relationship and supporting each other in front of the third party will feel good to both of you and set limits on the temptation for others to interfere. A united front will convey the message that you are a well-protected and cohesive team.

SIMPLE PHRASES to FORTIFY SUPPORT:
- say THANK YOU often
- say PLEASE always
- say I'M SORRY when you mean it
- say I MISS YOU if you do
- say I NEED HELP as often as necessary
- say I NOTICE THAT YOU... so they feel seen/heard
- say I APPRECIATE IT WHEN... so no one feels taken for granted
- say I LOVE YOU when you feel it

Loyalty to the relationship entails being kind to each other on a regular basis.

I Think She's Hungry

Learning how to prepare for, navigate, and live with high levels of distress can help the relationship withstand occasional misfires. With so much going on, it is hard to imagine that misunderstandings and unintended offenses would not occur! Even so, feelings can get hurt quickly when misguided instincts or anxiety leads to dismissive comments or behaviors. Think about how your partner will feel or react, in addition to how you feel, and it will influence what you say and how you say it. Collaborating to solve a problem will be more efficient than making a presumption that may be off the mark. If one partner tends to be the primary caregiver during the day, it can often feel that all decisions or problem-solving solutions default to them. Over time, this feels overwhelming. A good example of this is feeding, which tends to fall to one partner over the other. A simple presumption that feeding is the go-to answer might be perceived as an impulsive quick-fix or an attempt to avert responsibility. Regardless of the subject at hand, check in with your partner to see what might be needed before jumping to conclusions or misinterpreting cues that may not align with what your partner needs.

Sharing hands-on responsibilities is the **#1** expert recommendation to reset equilibrium when partners feel overwhelmed. Always consider the strengths & weaknesses of each partner.

ARE YOU SHARING

FEEDING TASKS?

NIGHTTIME TASKS?

BATHING TASKS?

DIAPER/DRESSING TASKS?

OTHER HOUSEHOLD TASKS?

? ——— ?

? ——— ?

OMG would you wake up please? I can't believe you can sleep through all of this noise. If the baby wakes up, I WILL SERIOUSLY DIVORCE YOU. I CANNOT DO BOTH KIDS AT ONCE. I. CAN. NOT. DO THIS.
Honey, go back to bed. Everything is fine.
shhhhhh... shhhhhh....

Wake Up Please

Quality sleep may be unattainable for a while. In the meantime, it will benefit both of you if, early on, you can establish fair and shared nighttime responsibilities (see page 53). Still, feelings of resentment can sneak in and are best dealt with directly. It is always in your best interest to let your partner know how you are feeling and begin a discourse on how you both might rearrange things to reduce resentment. This isn't easy for everyone, but it's important, nonetheless. Feeling alone and unsupported and keeping those negative feelings inside is a surefire way to sabotage your good relationship. Even if your partner is working outside the home, you are both tired and overwhelmed. While that may be true, the primary caregiver, who is awake much of the night, has a different kind of fatigue. In many ways, it's harder. Guilt and self-esteem issues may preclude the nighttime primary caregiver from asking for help. But together, the two of you should discuss how to create a reasonable and cooperative middle-of-the-night game plan that involves both of you.

BABY-RELATED SLEEP QUESTIONS:

- Is the baby monitor helping or impeding?
- Are you prioritizing rest/sleep? (Forgo the chores!)
- When your baby sleeps or naps, are you trying to close your eyes & rest for a minute?
- Are you giving yourself permission to do this differently?
- Are you trading off sleep duties with your partner?
- Are you discussing feelings of resentment & how to modify behavior?
- If you are able to nap, are you careful to time this so you don't disrupt your bedtime routine?
- Are you letting others help when feasible?

Take the Baby!

After a long day of childcare, just the sight of your partner can feel like an oasis in the desert. But your partner feels the stress of the "real" world, the world outside. They face traffic, deadlines, cranky and stressed adults, and the intense pressure from work life. To each of you, the other's stressors probably seem more desirable, and it can be difficult to determine the fair share of the house and baby workload. Moreover, what appears fair is subject to renegotiation. Both parents should share parenting tasks, regardless of where or how much they work. Each of you needs time and permission to decompress from the day before entering your second shift. Discuss and plan specific ways to unwind before relying on each other for relief.

Chapter 8

Mom Struggles

Just Feed the Baby

One of the biggest influences on a mom's satisfaction and confidence is her perception of partner support. Regarding breastfeeding, partners who express ambivalence, or seem only concerned with "what's best for the baby" and not Mom's experience as well, may inadvertently sabotage her experience as well as her self-esteem. While the choice between breast or bottle is debatable for some, what stands out as incontrovertible is that ultimately the two of you are on the same page.

Keep these points in mind as you traverse this delicate territory:

* Some situations can impinge on the ability and decision to breastfeed (e.g., inadequate milk supply, latching issues, poor infant weight gain, illness, etc.).

* While breastfeeding is beneficial to the health of both baby and mom, there is no evidence that their bond will be negatively impacted if the baby is not breastfed.

* Recent studies show that breastfeeding may not have the long-term impact on childhood as previously believed.

* Moms should not have to defend their decision to breastfeed or bottle feed. No shame. No stigma. Everyone should support a mother's feeding choice.

The World Can Be a Scary Place

The world, indeed, can be a very scary place sometimes. There are real threats based on perilous situations, but interpretations and perceptions are often subjective, and what worries one of you may not worry the other. Sometimes, the "silly," more ordinary worries are easy to discern and alleviate with reassurance. And often, the unsafe, scary ones are also easy to determine and, ultimately, agree upon. What is not so easy to distinguish is the huge range of imagined and perceived frightening possibilities that can cast a shadow on every family activity. Anxiety is universal. And, while you cannot always control your environment, you can gain control over your reactions and feelings. Remember, it's okay to be anxious. You can learn to be anxious *better*. Learning to tolerate and endure anxiety is a task all new parents must confront at some point to move forward together with greater joy and less tension in the air.

BREATHE in & out through your NOSE with LONG deep EXHALES

→ increases oxygen to the brain

'SPLASH COLD water on face or end shower with 30 seconds cold water.

→ As the body adjusts to the cold, "fight or flight" response slows down.

Gargle water before swallowing. HUM or SING.

→ muscles used to gargle, sing & hum stimulate the vagus nerve, interrupt fight or flight mode, & signal to your brain that all is well.

Actually, I Really Do Take Care of Everything

No two families do everything the same way. Chores are distributed differently. Personal preferences and favorite activities vary. Family customs, expectations, and cultural influences are different. If you want help, you have to relinquish your need and desire to have it done the way you want it done. Many primary caregivers, who really *do* do more than their share of the household and baby care duties, may be reflexively unwilling to let that go. It's almost as if opposing forces keep them doing it all, resenting it yet resisting help. If you do this, ask yourself: Do you want to do everything yourself? Do you want to be 100 percent in charge of the household? Can you accept that your partner might take care of a task differently than you would? Your partner is an equal adult who should not be viewed, by either of you, as your assistant.

BALANCE
division of labor

WHAT I DO

WHAT YOU DO

If You Only Knew What I Was Thinking: Scary Thoughts

In our first book, *Good Moms Have Scary Thoughts*, we filled the pages with unspoken, scary thoughts to illustrate how universal they are. All moms, all dads, all parents have disturbing, unwanted thoughts about harm coming to their babies. They can be about the baby's safety and health; they can be about your competency as a parent; they can be about the outside world harming or taking them. These unthinkable thoughts, while terribly unsettling for parents, are actually extremely common. Holding on to that intense level of anxiety and the guilt that goes along with these thoughts will heighten distress and prolong suffering. The truth is, if you find a safe place to speak where you feel unjudged and cared for, your anxiety will lessen. You will feel better when you let someone you trust know what you are thinking.

109

Either Way, I Feel Guilty

The return to work is complicated, and not everyone has a choice in the matter. Whether it's a choice or a necessity, this obliges both partners to care for the emotions stirred up in the process. Regardless of the circumstances that brought you to this point, that first day going back to work is sure to generate a ton of mixed emotions. You might feel guilty if you are relieved to go. Guilty if you dread going. Guilty that you are leaving your baby behind. Guilty that your baby squeals with delight when she sees her new caretaker. Guilty when you have to run home because the baby is sick. Guilty that you aren't able to run home when the baby is sick. The list goes on. Remind yourself that guilt will not help, and the decision to go back to work comes from a place of dedication, commitment, and strength.

CONVERSATION STARTERS
when seeking support from your partner:
• "I guess it's not surprising that I feel guilty. I don't want to feel this way. Can you say something to make me feel better about going back?"
• "Can you remind me that this is the right thing?"
• "You are okay about my returning to work, right?"
• "Do you know how hard this is for me? Can we talk about it?"
• "Can you remind me that I'm a GOOD MOM/DAD/PARENT?"

I Cannot Live This Way

Letting your partner know how bad you feel when your thoughts are dark and scary is both challenging and imperative. Moms with a history of depression and anxiety are at higher risk for symptoms of depression and anxiety again after having a baby. Sometimes it's hard to distinguish between simply having bad days and the beginning of a mood disorder that needs professional attention. If you trust your partner,* tell them the extent to which you are suffering. This will help you gain perspective, feel supported, and determine the next best step. If at any point you do not feel safe or have thoughts of hurting yourself, let your healthcare provider know or call 911. Suicidal thoughts mean that a serious depression has set in and requires medical attention. Find someone you feel safe with so you can reveal the nature of your thoughts and how bad you feel. Do not presume this will get better on its own. Do not let feelings of shame or embarrassment get in the way of getting the help you need.

*If you do not trust your partner enough to share the true nature of your suffering, we urge you to seek immediate professional support for your relationship and for yourself.

#Speak the secret

What is scaring you the most about the way you are feeling?

What is it that you need/want your partner to know about the way you are feeling? Be specific.

Who should you contact immediately for support & intervention?

Chapter 9

Dad Struggles

116

What Are We Gonna Do?

Money is tight. Priorities are shifting. Stress is high. Burnout is high. You may be working harder than ever to keep up with the rising cost of raising a child or finding dependable child care. You may be frustrated and exhausted by the lack of support from our current system. Research shows that half of US families with young children who looked for child care reported difficulty finding it, and nearly one million families never found the program they wanted! All parents, regardless of socioeconomic status, admit to strong opinions and high stress related to cutting costs, rearranging priorities, and making huge sacrifices in order to manage the cost of raising children and finding affordable childcare. You may never have anticipated such a daunting strain on your relationship. Sit down and have a financial conversation. Make a plan and stick to it. Assess your resources and the details of the immediate reality, as well as of the bigger, more long-term picture. Reevaluate financial priorities. Listen to each other. Be sure to attend to the emotions that may be lurking beneath the numbers and the frustration. After all, discussions about money are never just about money.

It's NOT YOUR FAULT that the SYSTEM is BROKEN. It is REASONABLE to feel STUCK & OVERWHELMED. Do your best to support each other & be on the same team.

I feel stuck!

Me too!

118

I Can't Get Those Images Out of My Head

Sometimes childbirth brings unexpected, serious complications for which no one feels adequately prepared. Even when the outcome is good, if either partner witnesses a real or perceived life-threatening event, there can be distressing and enduring consequences. Post-traumatic stress disorder (PTSD) is real and can show up in the birth parent or the partner if there is any emergency or trauma related to the birth experience. (There can also be birth trauma with no PTSD.) To be clear, it is not only the objective trauma itself; it is also how the experience is perceived. This may be especially true if either partner has a history of trauma, which may be triggered by any (even non-traumatic) birth experience. A difficult birth can result in vivid or intrusive thoughts/memories, unresolved anger/rage, hyperawareness, and feeling constantly under threat of something terrible happening. Partners may feel unprepared for the rapid sequence of unpredictable events. Ideally, all obstetric conversations and groundwork should include partners to make sure everyone is as informed as possible. Conversations and debriefing of the birth experience are often cast aside while attention is focused on how mom and baby are doing. When things settle down, it is important to discuss your experience together. This provides an outlet for any lingering distress and can help you both regroup and focus on your new family.

Could You Stop Telling Me What to Do and How to Do It?

While most couples do find their rhythm after a few months with a new baby, it is highly likely that resentments will pop up or mosey around your relationship for a while. When expectations are unfulfilled or assumptions are unfair, couples can be left feeling bitter and unheard. Acknowledging your feelings and expectations aloud can help you find workable solutions, but doing this when you are upset is neither easy nor advisable. Discussions should be authentic, non-blaming, and noncritical. It is easy to take things for granted when both of you are so busy and exhausted.

Couples who learn how to negotiate the real-time responsibility of new roles and new duties find that they can offset rising resentments by sharing this burden of responsibility and creating a sense of fairness. Talking is always a part of the solution. Just remember: *How* you express yourself often overrides *what* you actually say.

Points to keep in mind when you need/want to say what's hard to say:

1. Stay calm. Take a breath. Take a break if you need to.
2. Renounce your need to be right.
3. Suspend negativity.
4. Stop keeping score.
5. Stop pointing fingers.
6. Believe in each other and your relationship.

122

Am I Just Like My Dad?

Many dads say that they learned how to be a dad by growing up with one. Overidentification with the same sex parent can have an upside and a downside. Most men soon learn, just like moms do, that parenthood is a never-ending process of growth by trial and error, by making some mistakes, and by learning what works best as you go along. Complicated relationships with dysfunctional interactions, such as an absent father, a narcissistic father, or an alcoholic father, can be particularly challenging, and it won't help for either of you to make hurtful references to this. Instead, be mindful of any area of vulnerability and approach it with compassion. This will help soothe any wounds and pave the way for healthy expectations and achievements. Remember, you both are facing the opportunity to create your own new narrative.

In what ways would I like to repeat how my mother/father was?

_____

In what ways would I NOT like to repeat how my mother/father was?

_____

What is one thing I learned from my mother/father that can help me now?

_____

I Have to Stay Strong for My Family

The launch into fatherhood carries a shocking financial strain and immense responsibility of taking care of the family. Things can quickly spin out of control, leaving dads feeling inadequate and powerless. Dads who like to fix problems might be at greater risk for burnout and feelings of helplessness because so much of the early commotion cannot be fixed away. Despite current efforts to level social and gender norms, it has been found that heterosexual men and women tend to shift to traditional gender roles and attitudes following the birth of a first child. Cultural sexism looms large, and men tend to suppress their emotions and may be less inclined to ask for help. This pattern is not sustainable, and the buildup of emotional pressure can lead to relationship stress, sleeping difficulties, and/or depression. There is still widespread misperception among many men and women that asking for help is a sign of weakness.

To the contrary, asking for help is one of the healthiest things you can do for yourself. It comes from a place of self-awareness and the courage to be vulnerable. Asking for help will also increase connectivity with your partner and expand your emotional comfort zone. Try to get used to talking about how you feel. It is one of the best ways to recharge when feeling emotionally overloaded.

Let us help you put this into Words:

start with: Could we make some time to talk later when there are no babies or pets around to distract us? It's important to me.

- Something I've been feeling or thinking lately, but afraid to tell you, is _____
- One of the things I need most from you now is _____
- If I were to be honest with myself, I should admit that I'm _____
- This is hard to say, but _____
- Thank you for _____

Would My Kids Be Better Off without Me?

The stigma attached to mental health issues is pervasive. In particular, the stigma of mental health issues related to parenthood is widespread and keeps many struggling parents from getting the help they need. Dads, as well as moms, are forced to hide their suffering, which indirectly reinforces the inescapable myth that real men don't get depressed. But men do get depressed! Depression after childbirth occurs in roughly 8 to 10 percent of fathers. Depression in men tends to present itself differently than it does with women, often manifesting as rage, anger, irritability, insomnia, withdrawal, and coping through an increase in risky behaviors, such as drinking, gambling, drug use, working too long, or interest in relationships outside the marriage. Men need to continue to change the narrative and expectation that they are immune to emotional illnesses. They need to talk about how they are feeling. This is especially true for men who have a family or personal history of depression or anxiety. If the risk is there, pretending the symptoms will go away on their own may only exacerbate the suffering. Ideally, men should be screened for depression, just as their partners are, to make sure both parents receive the support they may need. If you don't like the way you are feeling, please seek professional support (see page 141). If you seek help early on, you will feel better, function better, and learn to cope with extraordinary stressors.

Chapter 10

This Is Us Now

When Worry Resides

Many parents can relate to the pervasive and chronic worry that invades their space after having a baby. When worry settles in, it can hijack your best intentions. Hypervigilance can be a good thing when we are aware of our environment and alert to potential dangers. However, it can also lead to anxious micromanaging, which is distressing for both partners. Whether it's an ingrained habit or a biological tendency, many mothers feel hard-wired to worry-well and to take on this added burden with both great pride and resentment. Most confess that they are more apt to pay attention to detail and get things done. In fact, it has been shown that women's brains respond to infant cries by quickly switching to attentive mode, while men's brains stay in a resting state. Of course, all parents worry tons as they put on their brave faces. Soon, immediate worries mutate into long-term fears and, before you know it, it's hard to know the difference between sensible concerns and excessive worries. As your confidence grows, worries become less overwhelming and your perspective evens out.

WHAT HELPS

- Talking about worries helps take their power away.
- Stick to your routine.
- Stay focused on the present moment.
- Entertain your brain with something fun or meaningful.
- BREATHE

Are We Okay?

Couples under constant scrutiny or endless analysis are bound to periodically crumble under the pressure. Even the healthiest couples have to make room for intermittent outbursts and random meltdowns that can, if handled well, help the brain reset and get back on track with greater bandwidth and fortitude. Couples who stay strong are ones who can accept these emotional flare-ups as part of the territory. Though these episodes are to be taken seriously, they are not taken personally. Partners should accept some degree of moodiness as long as it is acknowledged and can be replaced by a mutual expression of support. Couples who can reframe the negativity with humor, shared goals, or intentional deflection are more likely to experience the turbulence as transitory and less likely to interpret it as a threat to the relationship. When the couple's stamina for high level stress is weakened by (1) pre-existing unhappy relationship, (2) lack of insight or coping skills to weather the existing stressors, or (3) overriding mental health concerns, both partners need to decide whether having an objective professional could help them refocus and invest in the partnership. Therapy can help you both take care of the relationship when you are so busy taking care of everything else.

Many couples mistakenly believe that strong relationships can take care of themselves, often putting the relationship on the back burner.

Being intentional about your relationship, leaning in, making it a priority, will make everything else you do feel easier.

Cultivating Resilience

Rediscovering yourself as a couple can ground you both and revive feelings that have been set aside to make room for the much-loved and ever-present craziness of having a baby. One of the best things you can do to make those fleeting feelings last longer is put words to them (e.g., *This feels so good*). Research shows that when individuals practice gratitude or positive affirmations, they experience a surge of certain neurotransmitters in the brain, like dopamine and norepinephrine, which can improve mood. Paying attention to the moments that feel good will be self-rewarding and will help train your brain to focus on and experience more positivity. If something disappoints you, try re-framing your response to be more positive (e.g., *Well, that wasn't what I expected, but it will be better next time*). This can be hard if you're not used to thinking that way, but if you practice, it gets easier. Accepting your current state is a good place to start. Find something good, something meaningful, or something intentional about how you feel now. Practice mindful appreciation of even the smallest things that feel good to you. Negative feelings eventually pass. Try to find magic in the moment.

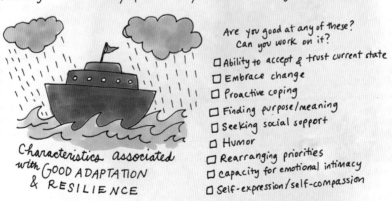

Characteristics associated with GOOD ADAPTATION & RESILIENCE

Are you good at any of these? Can you work on it?
- ☐ Ability to accept & trust current state
- ☐ Embrace change
- ☐ Proactive coping
- ☐ Finding purpose/meaning
- ☐ Seeking social support
- ☐ Humor
- ☐ Rearranging priorities
- ☐ capacity for emotional intimacy
- ☐ Self-expression/self-compassion

Finding Humor

Laughter is an underrated intervention that has been shown to open hearts and save relationships. Relying on your sense of humor is one of the best ways to enjoy each other's company, especially during times of stress. As long as you both think the same thing is funny! Sarcasm doesn't work, nonsensical disruptions can make things worse, and laughing when your partner doesn't think it's funny will not help. But if you know each other well and know what makes you both giggle, bring that good stuff into your home right now. Laughter is associated with tremendous benefits, such as increasing oxygen to your brain, releasing oxytocin, increasing endorphins, increasing and decreasing your heart rate, and improving your mood and your immune response. And there's more. The point is that your life is exceedingly stressful right now with good stress and not-so-good stress. The single best thing for you and your partner to do is to dive into this major life transition with as many personal resources as you can round up. Some you will cultivate along the way. Some you will read about and practice. And some, like your sense of humor, you already have. Find it. Use it. Enjoy it.

HUMOR INVENTORY

- ☐ Do you take yourself too seriously?
- ☐ Are you too busy to think something is funny?
- ☐ Do things that used to make you laugh no longer make you laugh?
- • Who makes you laugh the most? _____
- • Do you think you have a good sense of humor? _____
- • When was the last time you had a good belly laugh? _____
- • Does it feel good to laugh with your partner? _____
- • Can you think of something you can do to find that now? _____

Revisit Your Circle of Affection

In the introduction, we presented the circle of affection. Our hope is that the two of you have learned how to tap into those qualities that attracted you to each other in the first place and are beginning to practice skills to help insulate you from the endless distractions of parenthood. When you hear yourself asking *What about us?* that is the time to regroup and refocus on that special circle of just the two of you. With grit and fortitude, your relationship begins to reshape itself and, before you know it, the two of you have transformed into a family that works pretty darned well. Peace and harmony can be restored even though life is different. Something or someone will always insist you pay attention and nudge or even annihilate your circle of affection. You will be tempted to abandon the circle because, well, the scream for your company penetrates that sacred space. Keep in mind that the circle can sustain itself with the presence of pure intentions and loyalty to the relationship. This is a work in progress. As you travel through this incredible journey of good days and bad days, be clear about this—the strength and well-being of your secure connection within this circle can make the difference between couples who thrive and couples who struggle. Take good care of each other.

KEEP the MAGIC
* ALIVE *

* Do small things. often. *

* Find the good. *

* Give your partner the benefit of the doubt. *

* Be real, be open, be authentic, be forgiving, be tolerant. *

* Be Kind. Always. *

The single best
thing you can do for your
BABY:
PAY CLOSE ATTENTION
TO YOUR PARTNERSHIP.
HOLD 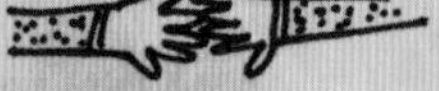 TIGHT to EACH OTHER
ASK FOR HELP WHEN YOU NEED IT,
and enjoy the ride.

Resources

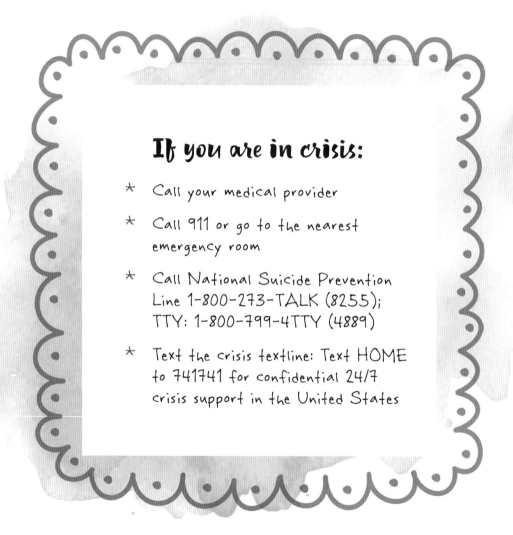

If you are in crisis:

* Call your medical provider

* Call 911 or go to the nearest emergency room

* Call National Suicide Prevention Line 1-800-273-TALK (8255); TTY: 1-800-799-4TTY (4889)

* Text the crisis textline: Text HOME to 741741 for confidential 24/7 crisis support in the United States

Looking For a Local Therapist?

The following organizations have searchable lists of therapists in and outside the US who are trained as postpartum specialists.

* The Postpartum Stress Center
  postpartumstress.com
  Searchable list: postpartumstress.com/get-help-2/
  where-can-i-get-help/professional-referrals

* Postpartum Support International
  postpartum.net
  Searchable list: postpartum.net/get-help/locations/
  united-states

Support and Information

The following specialized organizations provide advocacy, treatment, education, and support for perinatal women and their families, as well as the professionals who work with them.

* The Postpartum Stress Center
  postpartumstress.com

* Postpartum Support International
  postpartum.net
  800.944.4PPD (4773)

* 2020mom
  2020mom.org

* The Motherhood Center of NY
  themotherhoodcenter.com

* Seleni Institute
  seleni.org

* Massachusetts Child Psychiatry Access Program for Moms (MCPAP)
  mcpapformoms.org

* Massachusetts General Hospital Center for Women's Mental Health
  womensmentalhealth.org

* National Institute of Mental Health (NIMH)
  nimh.nih.gov/health/topics/women-and-mental-health/index.shtml

Additional Reading Material

For further information for yourself, your family, or your therapist, see Karen Kleiman's other books on postpartum depression and anxiety.

* *Good Moms Have Scary Thoughts: A Healing Guide to the Secret Fears of New Mothers.* Familius, 2019.

* *Dropping the Baby and Other Scary Thoughts: Breaking the Cycle of Unwanted Thoughts in Parenthood* (2nd Edition; with A. Wenzel, H. Waller and A. Adler-Mandel). Routledge, 2020.

* *The Art of Holding in Therapy: An Essential Intervention for Postpartum Depression and Anxiety.* Routledge, 2017.

* *Moods in Motion: A Coloring and Healing Book for Postpartum Moms.* Create Space, 2016.

* *Cognitive Behavioral Therapy and Perinatal Distress* (with A. Wenzel). Routledge, 2015.

* *Tokens of Affection: Reclaiming Your Marriage after Postpartum Depression* (with A. Wenzel). Routledge, 2014.

* *This Isn't What I Expected: Overcoming Postpartum Depression and Anxiety* (2nd Edition; with V. Raskin Davis). De Capo Books, 2013.

* Therapy and the Postpartum Woman: Notes on Healing Postpartum Depression for Clinicians and the Women Who Seek Their Help. Routledge, 2009.

* What Am I Thinking: Having a Baby after Postpartum Depression. Xlibris, 2005.

* The Postpartum Husband: Practical Solutions for Living with Postpartum Depression. Xlibris, 2001.

We also recommend these excellent books for couples:

* *Becoming Us* by Elly Taylor (Three Turtles Press, 2014).

* *And Baby Makes Three: The Six-Step Plan For Preserving Marital Intimacy And Rekindling Romance After Baby Arrives* by John Gottman and Julie Schwartz Gottman (Harmony, 2008).

* *The Seven Principles for Making Marriage Work* by John M. Gottman and Nan Silver (Harmony, 2015).

Our recommendations for best apps for relaxation and mindfulness practice:

* Headspace

* Calm

* Ten Percent Happier Meditation

* The Breathing App

References

Introduction

* Beck, C. 2001. "Predictors of Postpartum Depression: An Update." *Nursing Research* 50(5): 275-285.

* Doss, B.; Rhoades, G.; Stanley, S.; and Markman, H. 2009. "The Effect of the Transition to Parenthood on Relationship Quality: An 8-Year Prospective Study." *Journal of Personality and Social Psychology* 96(3): 601-619. https://doi.org/10.1037/a0013969.

* Gottman, J. and Gottman, J. 2008. *And Baby Makes Three: The Six-Step Plan for Preserving Marital Intimacy and Rekindling Romance after Baby Arrives.* New York: Harmony Press.

* Kleiman, K. 2019. *Good Moms Have Scary Thoughts: A Healing Guide to the Secret Fears of New Mothers.* Sanger, CA: Familius.

Chapter 1

* Hairston, I.; Handelzalts, J.; Lehman-Inbar, T.; and Kovo M. 2019. "Mother-Infant Bonding Is Not Associated with Feeding Type: A Community Study Sample." *BMC Pregnancy Childbirth* 19(1): 125.

* Mannion, C. A.; Hobbs, A. J.; McDonald, S. W.; and Tough, S. C. 2013. "Maternal Perceptions of Partner Support during Breastfeeding." *International Breastfeeding Journal*, 8(1), 4.

* Kaiser Permanente Division of Research. 2008. "One in Three Women Has Pelvic Floor Disorder." *ScienceDaily*, March 5, 2008. www.sciencedaily.com/releases/2008/03/080302150723.htm.

* Saxbe, D.; Schetter, C.; Simon, C.; Adam, E.; and Shalowitz, M. 2017. "High Paternal Testosterone May Protect Against Postpartum Depressive Symptoms in Fathers, but Confer Risk to Mothers and Children." *Hormones and Behavior* 95: 103–112. doi:10.1016/j.yhbeh.2017.07.014.

Chapter 3

* Gettler L.; McDade, T.; Feranil, A.; and Kuzawa, C. 2011. "Longitudinal Evidence That Fatherhood Decreases Testosterone in Human Males." *Proceedings of the National Academy of Sciences of the United States of America* 27;108 (39): 16194–9.

Chapter 4

* Doss, B. and Rhoades, G. 2017. "The Transition to Parenthood: Impact on Couples' Romantic Relationships." *Current Opinion in Psychology* 13: 25–28. doi:10.1016/j.copsyc.2016.04.003.

* Graham, A.; Fisher, P.; and Pfeifer, J. 2013. "What Sleeping Babies Hear: An fMRI Study of Interparental Conflict and Infants' Emotional Processing." *Psychological Science* 24 (5): 782–789.

* Kleiman, K. and Wenzel, A. 2014. *Tokens of Affection: Reclaiming Your Marriage after Postpartum Depression.* New York: Routledge.

* Shapiro, A.; Gottman, J.; and Carrere, S. 2000. "The Baby and the Marriage: Identifying Factors That Buffer against Decline in Marital Satisfaction after the First Baby Arrives." *Journal of Family Psychology* 14 (1): 59–70.

Chapter 5

* The Society of Reproductive Surgeons. n.d. "FAQ Quick Facts about Infertility." Retrieved August 16, 2020, from https://www.reprodsurgery.org/srs/home?ssopc=1.

Chapter 8

* Colen, C. and Ramey, D. 2014. "Is Breast Truly Best? Estimating the Effects of Breastfeeding on Long-Term Child Health and Well-Being in the United States Using Sibling Comparisons." *Social Science & Medicine* 109: 55–65. https://doi.org/10.1016/j.socscimed.2014.01.027.

* Hairston, Handelzalts, Lehman-Inbar, and Kovo. 2019. Mother-Infant Bonding.

* Kleiman, K.; Wenzel, A.; Waller, H.; and Adler-Mandel, A. 2020. *Dropping the Baby and Other Scary Thoughts: Breaking the Cycle of Unwanted Thoughts in Parenthood*, 2nd ed. New York: Routledge.

Chapter 9

* Baxter, J.; Bucher, S.; Perales, F.; and Western, M. 2014. "A Life-Changing Event: First Births and Men's and Women's Attitudes to Mothering and Gender Divisions of Labor." *Social Forces* 93(3): 989–1014.

* Scarff J. 2019. "Postpartum Depression in Men." *Innovations in Clinical Neuroscience* 16(5–6): 11–14.

* Schochet, L. 2019. "The Child Care Crisis Is Keeping Women Out of the Workforce." Center for American Progress. Retrieved November 23, 2020, from www.americanprogress.org/ issues/early-childhood/reports/2019/03/28/467488/child-care-crisis-keeping-women-workforce/.

Chapter 10

* Bornstein, M.; Putnick, D.; Rigo, P.; Esposito, G.; Swain, J.; Suwalsky, J.; Su, X.; Du, X.; Zhang, K.; Cote, L.; De Pisapia, N.; and Venuti, P. 2017. "The Neurobiology of Culturally Common Maternal Responses to Infant Cry." *Proceedings of the National Academy of Sciences* 114 (45): E9465-E9473.

* Doidge, N. 2007. *The Brain That Changes Itself: Stories of Personal Triumph from the Frontiers of Brain Science.* New York: Penguin.

* Fry, W. 1992. "The Physiological Effects of Humor, Mirth, and Laughter." *Journal of the American Medical Association* 267: 1857-1858.

About the Author

Karen Kleiman is a well-known international maternal mental-health expert with over thirty-five years of experience as a psychotherapist, teacher, and writer. As an advocate and author of several groundbreaking books on postpartum depression and anxiety, including *Good Moms Have Scary Thoughts*, her pioneering work has been featured on the internet and within the perinatal mental health community for decades. In 1988, Karen founded The Postpartum Stress Center, a treatment and training facility for prenatal and postpartum depression/anxiety disorders where she treats individuals and couples. Moms and dads can find support from The Postpartum Stress Center (postpartumstress.com) on Facebook, Twitter, and Instagram which includes their #speakthesecret campaign to bust the stigma of perinatal intrusive thoughts.

About the Illustrator

Molly McIntyre is an artist, illustrator, and animator living in Brooklyn, New York, with her family. Her work has been featured in the Netflix series *Worn Stories*, the book *Good Moms Have Scary Thoughts* (Karen Kleiman, Familius), *Bitch* magazine, Everyday Feminism, Scary Mommy, and *Psychology Today*, and shown in exhibitions throughout the US and in Japan.

#speakthesecret

About Familius

Visit Our Website: www.familius.com

Familius is a global trade publishing company that publishes books and other content to help families be happy. We believe that the family is the fundamental unit of society and that happy families are the foundation of a happy life. We recognize that every family looks different, and we passionately believe in helping all families find greater joy. To that end, we publish books for children and adults that invite families to live the Familius Ten Habits of Happy Family Life: love together, play together, learn together, work together, talk together, heal together, read together, eat together, give together, and laugh together. Founded in 2012, Familius is located in Sanger, California.

Connect

Facebook: www.facebook.com/familiustalk
Twitter: @familiustalk, @paterfamilius1
Pinterest: www.pinterest.com/familius
Instagram: @familiustalk

FAMILIUS

The most important work you ever do
will be within the walls of your own home.